The Seven
Spiritual Laws
for Parents

Books by
DEEPAK CHOPRA

◆

The Seven Spiritual Laws for Parents

Guiding Your Children to Success and Fulfillment

DEEPAK CHOPRA

Harmony Books

NEW YORK

Published by Harmony Books, a division of Crown Publishers, Inc., 201 East 50th Street, New York, New York 10022. Member of the Crown Publishing Group.

Design by Lynne Amft

Random House, Inc. New York, Toronto, London, Sydney, Auckland

http://www.randomhouse.com/

HARMONY and colophon are trademarks of Crown Publishers, Inc.

Printed in the United States of America

Library of Congress Cataloging-in-Publication Data
Chopra, Deepak.
   The seven spiritual laws for parents : guiding your children
to success and fulfillment / by Deepak Chopra. — 1st ed.
     p. cm.
   1. Child rearing—Religious aspects. 2. Parenting—
Religious aspects.   3. Children—Religious life.
4. Children—Conduct of life. 5. Religious education of
children.   6. Spiritual life. I. Title.
HQ769.3.C455 1997
649'.1—dc21   97-19609
                                                    CIP

ISBN 0-609-60077-X

10 9 8 7 6 5 4 3 2 1

First Edition

To my wife, Rita;
to my children,
Mallika and Gautama;
and to my parents,
Krishan and Pushpa,
all of whom taught me
the true meaning of parenting

Contents

Acknowledgments

Deepest thanks to my family, which has always supported me and taught me the true meaning of success; to my support staff at The Chopra Center for Well Being in La Jolla, California, and at Infinite Possibilities in Massachusetts; to my extended family at Harmony—especially Peter Guzzardi, Patty Eddy, Tina Constable, and Chip Gibson; and finally, as always, to Muriel Nellis, who has been the godmother of all my literary endeavors.

Introduction

After my book *The Seven Spiritual Laws of Success* was published, the response was immediate and very beautiful: thousands of people who read the book began to practice in their daily lives the principles that Nature uses to create everything in material existence.

In time I received requests from many of these people who also happened to be parents. Their requests took many forms, but they echoed a single theme: "As much as I have benefited from living these spiritual laws, I wish I had learned them years ago. The value of such principles as giving, having no resistance, and trusting in the universe to fulfill my desires seems obvious now, but it wasn't at first. It was a struggle to break the destructive habits that I grew up with. As a parent I don't want my own chil-

Introduction

dren to learn the same bad habits and later have to go through the same pain of having to change. How can I make sure that doesn't happen?"

I wrote this new book to answer these requests, extending *The Seven Spiritual Laws* specifically to parents. It will show anyone who wants to interpret the spiritual laws for children how to do that in terms a child can understand and apply. My approach here is founded on the belief that every parent needs tools to raise children with a true understanding of the workings of Nature and consciousness.

Everyone in the world wants something; everyone in the world has desires. Children need to know, from the beginning, that desire is the most basic drive in human nature. It is the energy of the spirit. When we grow up and seek answers to profound questions or set out to solve immensely challenging issues in our personal lives, what we work with is the same natural desire that made us curious children, nothing more. The seeker is the child who has gone from needing a parent's love to needing God's, from wanting toys to wanting infinite creativity. In this

Introduction

book I will try to show parents how their children can best fulfill their desires and successfully attain what they want in life. And I will do my best to explain spiritual concepts so that a child can understand them. But this is not simply a book aimed at children, since what children need to know is only a modified form of what adults need to know as well.

With all its worship of material success, society has missed a profound truth: success depends on who you are, not what you do. Being or essence or spirit—call it by any name you want—lies at the source of all achievement in life. But Being is very abstract, so people see it more as an idea than as something real and useful. Nevertheless, if we examine the oldest traditions of human wisdom, we find certain fixed, knowable, reliable principles by which spirit unfolds from eternal Being into everyday life.

Some people may have difficulty understanding how spiritual laws could be of such value in daily life yet remain in obscurity for so many centuries. By analogy, electricity did not enter general awareness before the lightbulb, despite the fact that the entire universe has been permeated with electrical energy since the dawn of creation. Being or spirit or essence is invisible, too, yet it affects daily life in a tremendous way. The invisible intelligence behind the visible universe operates through Seven Spiritual Laws. Again by analogy, if the laws of electricity hadn't been discovered, the practical applications of electricity would never have been available to us.

Now more than ever, in this age of violence and confusion, there is an urgent need for parents to take on the role of spiritual teachers to their children. The laws behind Nature's working are not private. They apply to everyone and everything. Therefore, understanding these laws is not just a way to help a few people; it is vital for our society and even for our civilization. If a critical mass of our children are raised to practice the Seven Spiritual Laws, our whole civilization will be transformed. Love and compassion, which are so often trivialized these days, can become the natural breath and life of everyone's existence. We owe it to the world, I believe, to ensure that as many children as possible grow up knowing what spiritual reality is.

Spirit has always been elusive. An ancient Indian

Introduction

scripture informs us that a knife cannot cut It, water cannot wet It, wind cannot blow It away, the sun cannot dry It up. Every molecule in the universe is permeated with Being; every thought you have, every bit of information that reaches you through your five senses is nothing but Being. But Being can be overlooked, since it is completely silent, like a master choreographer that never joins the dance. In Being we are all upheld; we take our very breath and life from it, yet it is something our own parents taught us little about.

We can all be forgiven our lack of knowledge about spirit, and we can teach ourselves the Seven Spiritual Laws with the same enthusiasm as we teach our children. More than anything else, this has been the guiding ideal behind this book.

PART ONE

Parenting

and the

Gift of Spirit

After all, what is God?
An eternal Child playing an eternal game
in the eternal garden.

SRI AUROBINDO

The deepest desire in a parent's heart is to see one's child achieve success in life, yet how many of us realize that the most direct way to success is through spirit? In our society we don't usually make that connection—quite the opposite. We teach our children how to survive, how to behave in order to earn our approval, how to defend themselves, how to compete, how to persist against disappointment, obstacles, and setbacks. Although believing in God is often considered a good thing, spirit has traditionally been set apart from success in daily life. This is a mistake, and it has had a profound effect on all our lives, from childhood on.

Many people assume without question that success is essentially material, that it can be measured in money, prestige, or an abundance of possessions. These can certainly play a role, but having such things is no guarantee of success. The success we want our children to achieve has to be defined in many nonmaterial ways as well. It should include the ability to love and have compassion, the capacity to feel joy and spread it to others, the security of knowing that one's life serves a purpose, and finally, a sense of connection to the creative power of the universe. All of these constitute the spiritual dimension of success, the dimension that brings inner fulfillment.

If the meaning of your life unfolds to you every day, in simplicity and wonder, you have achieved success—which means, in a profound way, that every baby is born a success. Every child's ability to feel wonder in the face of everyday existence is the surest proof we have that Nature wants us to be successful. It is in our own nature to respond to life with joy. The seeds of God are inside us. When we make

Parenting and the Gift of Spirit

the journey of spirit, we water these divine seeds. The good life merely reflects our inner intention. In time the flowers of God bloom within and around us, and we begin to witness and know the miracle of the divine wherever we go.

Our responsibility as parents is therefore to place our children firmly on the journey of spirit. This is the best thing we can do to ensure their success in life, better than giving them money, a secure home, or even love and affection. I ask you to consider this spiritual notion of parenting, different though it may be from how you see your role now.

To bring about this new way of parenting we need practical principles to teach our children. The principles I have in mind were introduced in my earlier book as the Seven Spiritual Laws of Success. In order to bring about a connection with spirit, a knowledge of spiritual law is essential. When we practice spiritual laws, we put ourselves in harmony with Nature. Any other way of living leads to strain and struggle. Success achieved on the basis of struggle may bring good things to us, but the inner *fulfillment* we seek from these things will be lacking.

In adult language the Seven Spiritual Laws are stated as follows:

FIRST LAW: *The Law of Pure Potentiality*
The source of all creation is pure consciousness . . . pure potentiality seeking expression from the unmanifest to the manifest.

SECOND LAW: *The Law of Giving*
In our willingness to give that which we seek, we keep the abundance of the universe circulating in our lives.

THIRD LAW: *The Law of "Karma"*
When we choose actions that bring happiness and success to others, the fruit of our karma is happiness and success.

FOURTH LAW: *The Law of Least Effort*
Nature's intelligence functions with effortless ease . . . with carefreeness, harmony, and love. When we harness these forces, we create success with the same effortless ease.

Parenting and the Gift of Spirit

FIFTH LAW: *The Law of Intention and Desire*

Inherent in every intention and desire is the mechanics for their fulfillment . . . in the field of pure potentiality, intention and desire have infinite organizing power.

SIXTH LAW: *The Law of Detachment*

In our willingness to step into the unknown, the field of all possibilities, we surrender ourselves to the creative mind that orchestrates the dance of the universe.

SEVENTH LAW: *The Law of "Dharma"*

When we blend our unique talent with service to others, we experience the ecstasy and exultation of our own spirit, which is the ultimate goal of all goals.

Whether you call these "laws" or "principles" is not important. They are laws inasmuch as they govern the unfolding of spirit as it moves from the invisible world of the soul to the visible world of matter.

They are principles inasmuch as we can take them to heart and apply them the same way we would apply a principle like telling the truth or being fair.

Why do we need such principles? Why not simply teach our children to love God and be good?

The answer is that the Seven Spiritual Laws put a person in touch with the mechanics of Nature. When you consciously align your life with spiritual law, you are asking the universe to support you with success and abundance. This is the key to becoming aware of your own Being and using its infinite power. The earlier someone is taught how to live in the most effortless, harmonious, and creative way, the more likely it is that all of life will bring success. This is what we are asked to pass on to our children, and if we can do it, nothing brings more joy and pride.

Every spiritual tradition contains some version of these seven laws, but they emerge in their purest form from the ancient Vedic tradition of India, which articulated them more than five thousand years ago. The Seven Spiritual Laws serve one vision, as follows:

Human beings are made of body, mind, and

spirit. Of these, spirit is primary, for it connects us to the source of everything, the eternal field of consciousness. The more connected we are, the more we will enjoy the abundance of the universe, which has been organized to fulfill our wishes and desires. Only in a state of disconnection do we suffer and struggle. The divine intention is for every human being to enjoy unlimited success.

Success, therefore, is supremely natural.

Children and Spirit—The Teaching of Innocence

The language of the Seven Spiritual Laws has to be different when spoken to a child, less abstract. Fortunately, the same laws can be phrased so that even a young child is able to carry them around in mind and heart:

> First Law:
> *Everything is possible.*

SECOND LAW:
If you want to get something, give it.

THIRD LAW:
When you make a choice, you change the future.

FOURTH LAW:
Don't say no—go with the flow.

FIFTH LAW:
Every time you wish or want, you plant a seed.

SIXTH LAW:
Enjoy the journey.

SEVENTH LAW:
You are here for a reason.

On the day I wrote down these simple sayings, I didn't pause to think about them much, but afterward it hit me: if I had been taught just these seven sentences as a child, my life would have been profoundly different. I would have known something

precious and practical at the same time, something
that would not have faded as a childhood lesson but
would have ripened into mature spiritual understanding year by year.

A child raised with spiritual skills will be able to
answer the most basic questions about how the universe works; she will understand the source of creativity both within and outside herself; she will be
able to practice nonjudgment, acceptance, and
truth, which are the most valuable skills anyone can
possess for dealing with other people; and she will
be free from the crippling fear and anxiety about the
meaning of life that is the secret dry rot inside the
hearts of most adults, whether they can admit it
or not.

*The deepest nurturing you can give your child is
spiritual nurturing.*

I am not talking about forcing hard-and-fast
rules on your children, the way we teach them to be
good or risk being punished. Each of the Seven Spiritual Laws should be conveyed not as a rule or rigid
precept but as *your own way of looking at life.* As a
parent, you will teach much more effectively by who

you are, not what you say. This itself is part of the spiritual perspective.

Every child has a spiritual life already. This is because every child is born into the field of infinite creativity and pure awareness that is spirit. But not every child knows that this is true. Spirit must be cultivated; it must be nourished and encouraged. If it is, then a child's innocent spirit grows up to be strong enough to withstand the harsh realities of an often unspiritual world.

Losing touch with spirit does nothing to the infinite field of creativity, which is beyond harm, but it can do much to damage a person's chances in life. With spirit we are all children of the cosmos; without it we are orphaned and set adrift.

Let's take an example. The Seventh Law says, "You are here for a reason." A child's reason for being here can be put in simple, everyday terms, such as

How did I make a difference today?

What talent did I uncover?

What came to me—a gift, a lesson, a beautiful experience—that made me feel special?

However, a child who was taught from the age of
three or four "You are here for a reason" would face
a very different future. Such a child would see the
search for meaning in life as a natural thing, the spiritual equivalent of learning your ABCs. There would
be no years of postponement, followed by desperate
inner turmoil. "Why am I here?" doesn't have to be
a fearsome existential question. It is the most joyful
exploration a person can undertake, and we do our
children an immense favor by presenting it as such.
A child who paid attention to just this one principle
would have a far richer life—a more successful life—
than countless adults for whom "spirit" and "God"
remain forever locked in a world of abstraction.

Real spiritual growth changes a person in a para-
doxical way. It brings understanding at the same
time as it preserves innocence. As parents we are
sorely tempted to distance ourselves from childhood. We do this by seeming to know more about
life, when in fact we have usually just experienced
more. We have gotten good at knowing the rules and
avoiding punishment, at hiding our weakness with a
show of strength, at never letting slip the mask of

invulnerability. There is no better recipe for destroying a child's innocence than to destroy our own.

In the eyes of spirit, everyone is innocent, in all senses of the word. Because you are innocent, you have not done anything that merits punishment or divine wrath. You are new-made every day. You are a receptor for experience that never ceases to inspire delight and wonder. There is only one spiritual difference between the innocence of children and the innocence of grown-ups: we grown-ups are innocent *with understanding*—and that is what we are meant to impart, while retaining the pure, fresh, pristine quality that comes with true knowledge.

How to Start

From the day your baby is born, you are a teacher of spirit. If you create an atmosphere of trust, openness, non-judgment, and acceptance, those qualities will be absorbed as the qualities of spirit.

In a perfect world, parenting would come down to one sentence: *Show only love, be only love.* But in the world we all cope with, children grow up to face much non-loving behavior, primarily outside the home but sometimes within it as well. Rather than worry about whether you embody enough love to qualify as a spiritual teacher, look upon spirituality as a skill in living, since that is what it is. I believe in imparting these skills as early as possible by whatever means a child can understand.

INFANT, 0–1 YR.

KEY WORDS: *Love, affection, attention*

Fortunately for our generation, the misconception that children need to be trained and disciplined from the cradle has been discarded. An infant is pure spiritual gold. Cherishing her innocence is the way to find the path back to our own. So in a very important way it is the parent who sits at the feet of the baby. Spiritual bonding with your infant comes through touching, holding, providing security from harm, playing, and giving attention. Without these "primitive" responses from the environment, the human organism cannot flourish; it will languish and wither as surely as a flower deprived of sunlight.

TODDLER, 1 — 2 YRS.

KEY WORDS: *Freedom, encouragement, respect*

This is the stage in which the child is first gaining ego. Here I mean *ego* in the simplest sense of "self," a conviction of "I am." This is a precarious time, for the toddler is testing detachment from the parent for the first time. The lure of freedom and curiosity pulls in one direction, but there is fear and insecurity pulling in the other. Not all experiences of being on one's own are pleasant. It is therefore up to the parent to communicate a spiritual lesson without which no child can truly grow into independent selfhood: that the world is safe.

Feeling safe as an adult means that some time before the age of two, you were not conditioned by fear; you were encouraged instead to expand without limit, to value freedom despite the occasional wound that can come when a child bumps into the things of this world. Falling down is not the same as failing; being hurt is not the same as deciding that the world is dangerous. Hurting is nothing more than Nature's way of telling a child where the boundaries lie—pain exists to show a toddler where "me" begins and ends, to help a child avoid potential dangers like burning oneself or falling downstairs.

When parents distort this natural learning process, the result is a sense of psychological pain, which is not what Nature intended. Psychological pain sets up boundaries that you cannot cross without feeling deep anxiety about your state of being. If a child connects being hurt with being bad, weak, unable to cope, or constantly surrounded by threat, there is no room left for inner spiritual growth. For without a sense of safety, spirit remains out of reach; one is forever trying simply to feel secure in this world, yet that security cannot be achieved without overcoming the imprints of early childhood.

PRESCHOOL, 2–5 YRS.

KEY WORDS: *Deserving, exploring, approving*

This stage is all about building a child's sense of self-esteem. Self-esteem provides readiness to go outside the family to encounter the big, wide world. It is identified with tasks and challenges. Until the age of two or three, a toddler has no responsibility for tasks—simply to play and be joyous is enough. There is no spiritual need for anything but to nurture the delight of the child's self as it unfolds to a fresh, new world.

With toilet training and learning to feed himself, a toddler begins to realize that "I am" can expand to "I can." Once the ego realizes this, there is no stopping a two-year-old. He thinks he has the whole world—and certainly everyone in his family—by the tail. "I" is like a power generator just plugged in, and what makes the twos terrible is that the newly born ego surges with power in an undisciplined way. Shouting, screaming, running around, wielding the all-powerful word *no!* and generally trying to rule reality by sheer will—this is exactly what should be going on at this stage.

Spiritually, the value of the preschool stage is that power *is* spiritual—only the distortion of power leads to problems. So rather than try to curb your child's rush to power, you need to channel it into tasks and challenges that teach balance. Without being put into balance, the power hunger of a preschooler will run into grief, because her experience is largely the illusion of power. A ranting two-year-old is still a very tiny, vulnerable, unformed person. In our love for the child, we allow the illusion to exist, because we want her to grow up a strong, capable person who feels up to any challenge that comes along. This sense of self-esteem won't develop if the feeling of being powerful is shut down or repressed at this stage.

KINDERGARTEN—EARLY PRIMARY SCHOOL, 5–8 YRS.

KEY WORDS: *Giving, sharing, non-judgment, acceptance, truth*

The key words that apply to the first years of school begin to sound more social. Of course there are many other words, for once a child has been experiencing the world for five years, the brain is so complex and active that countless concepts are being absorbed and tested. I also don't mean to imply that sharing, giving, and telling the truth can be ignored before this age, but the critical aspect of this stage is that abstract concepts can now begin to be assimilated. The concrete mind of the infant, which has not understood reasons for your behavior, only how it feels, now blossoms into a capacity for accepting realities beyond "I am," "I want," and "I come first."

Giving is how, at any age, we show that we empathize with needs outside ourselves. If giving is seen as loss—I have to give something up so that you can have it—the spiritual lesson of this stage has not been taught. Giving, in spiritual terms, means "I give to you without loss because you are part of me." A young child cannot fully grasp this idea, but he can *feel* it. Children don't just *want* to share—they love to share. They feel the warmth that comes from reaching beyond ego boundaries to include another person in their world; no act is more intimate, and therefore no act feels so blissful.

The same holds for telling the truth. We lie in order to remain safe, to avert danger of punishment. Fear of punishment implies inner tension, and even if a lie actually does protect us from perceived danger, it rarely if ever relieves this inner tension. Only the truth can do that. When a young child is taught that telling the truth will result in a good feeling, she has taken the first step toward realizing that truth has a spiritual quality. It isn't necessary to use punishment. If you foster the attitude of "tell the truth or you'll be in trouble," you have taught something spiritually false. A child who is tempted to lie is under the influence of fear; if truth gets associated with this fear, then the mind quite logically tries to get better at seeming to tell the truth.

In either case, the child is forced to act better than he feels he actually is. Learning to act out what others demand is a sure recipe for spiritual destruction. Your child must feel that "this is what I myself want to do."

Parenting and the Gift of Spirit

OLDER CHILDREN, 8–12 YRS.

KEY WORDS: *Independent judgment, discrimination, insight*

For many parents this stage is the most enjoyable because this is when children develop personality and independence. They think on their own, come up with hobbies, likes and dislikes, enthusiasms— the rush of discovery is on its trajectory to things that may last for life, such as a love of science or art. The key spiritual concepts here are all in line with this exciting phase.

Although it sounds dry, "discrimination" is a beautiful quality of the soul. It goes far beyond telling right from wrong. In these years the nervous system itself is capable of sustaining subtle impressions of great depth and importance to the future. A ten-year-old child is capable of wisdom, and for the first time that most delicate of gifts—personal insight—comes about. The child can see and judge through her own eyes; she no longer has to receive the world secondhand from adults.

This is therefore the first stage in which anything

like a spiritual law can be grasped conceptually. Before this, the idea of a law just seems like a rule you have to obey or at least pay attention to. Instead of using the word *law,* a parent might be conveying helpful insights into "how things work" or "why things turn out the way they do" or "how to do it so it feels good." These are more concrete, experience-centered ways of teaching. By age ten or so, however, abstract reasoning takes an independent turn, and the true teacher is now experience, not an authority figure. Why this happens is a spiritual mystery, for experience has been there since birth, but for some reason the world suddenly speaks to a child; she can grasp the upwelling within herself of why something is true or not, why truth and love matter.

EARLY TEENS, 12–15 YRS.

KEY WORDS: *Self-awareness, experimentation, responsibility*

Childhood ends with early adolescence, traditionally a trying and difficult time. For children, innocence suddenly runs into puberty and the arrival of needs that parents can no longer fill. For parents, the real-ization dawns that they must let go of their children and trust that they are capable of dealing with a world of responsibility and pressure that the parents themselves may have barely learned to adjust to without insecurity.

What is critical is that by now the lessons of childhood have borne either sweet or bitter fruit. The child who can go forth imprinted with genuine spiritual knowledge will reflect her parents' pride and trust; the child who stumbles into confusion, reckless experimentation, and peer pressure is like-wise reflecting the hidden confusion of his up-bringing. Adolescence is notoriously a time of self-consciousness, but it can also be a time of self-awareness.

Experimentation is a natural part of the transi-tion from childhood, but it doesn't have to be reck-less and destructive. Now the issue is whether the child has an inner self that can be used as a guide. This inner self is the silent voice that has the power to choose between right and wrong based upon a deep knowingness about life. This knowingness is not confined to any age. A newborn baby has it as fully as a mature adult. The difference is that the mature adult has cultivated behavior that follows the inner guide—if you have taught your child to heed her own silence, there is no peril in letting her go out into the world no longer a child. In fact, it is a joyful experience (if occasionally a nerve-racking one) to watch her grow in self-awareness by experimenting with the vast array of choices life has to offer.

Teaching Right from Wrong

Because we have all grown up in a society that places so little real value on spiritual life, it can be confusing to consider what being a spiritual teacher to your child means. How does this differ, for instance, from merely being a good, loving parent? To demonstrate, let's take a crucial issue that arises with all children: teaching the distinction between right and wrong.

I think we'd all agree that the old practice of teaching through punishment and reprimand is to be avoided. Setting yourself up as a punitive authority only emphasizes moral dilemmas you have not solved for yourself. Children quickly detect the gap between what we say as parents and how we behave. They may learn to obey us out of fear of punishment, but at the emotional level, they intuit that a parent who has to use threats and coercion is not a model of what "good" should mean.

Yet we all know that, despite our best intentions, times do arise when it is tempting to punish children out of sheer exasperation and frustration. If we examine these moments closely, we realize that we are using punishment to resolve issues that aren't resolved in our own hearts. Do we really believe it is possible to be truly good all the time? Do we fear a God who will exact punishment on us if we are bad? Is evil a force we feel helpless before, uncertain if goodness can even stand up to it in this world, much less triumph?

The frailties of our own spiritual lives come out in the way we decide to parent. There is no escaping this, and even when you try to be loving and gentle with your children, there are bound to be times when your own doubts will be triggered. Being a spiritual teacher goes beyond how you behave—you are here to impart real truths about the nature of spiritual life.

The easiest way to teach the meaning of spirit is to create an atmosphere in which spirit is breathed in as love. To have a baby is such an act of grace that every parent wants to return the gift many times over. This is an impulse I have felt intimately. I could summon the confidence to write this book because my own two children allowed me to learn the Seven Spiritual Laws through them. Because of their innocence children are ruthless teachers of truth and love. Unless you parent in the total spirit of love, it doesn't matter what laws you think you are teaching—they will become just lifeless rules that your child will discard as soon as there is no longer an authority to demand obedience.

From very early in our children's lives, my wife and I found that we were instinctively following certain practices that only later jelled into principles:

• We taught our children to take spirit as a reality, to believe in an infinite source of love that held them dearly. This was our working definition of God.

Parenting and the Gift of Spirit

- We put no pressure on them to achieve conventional success. This was our way of telling them that the universe cherished them for who they are, not for what they do.

- We never felt the need to punish them, although we let our children know very honestly when we were disappointed, angry, or hurt. This was our way of teaching by reflection instead of rules.

- We always remembered that our children were gifts from the universe and let them know that we felt that way. We told them how privileged and honored we felt to help raise them. We didn't own or possess them. We didn't project our own expectations onto them. We never felt the need to compare them—for good or bad—with anyone else. This was our way of making them feel complete within themselves.

- We told them that they had gifts that could change other people's lives. We also told them that they could change and create anything they wanted in their own lives.

- We told them very early on the kind of success that matters—to bring about worthwhile goals that were meaningful to them, goals that brought them joy. This was the best way we knew of to bring joy and meaning to others.

- Finally, we encouraged their dreams. This was our way of telling our children to trust their own desires, the royal road to the inner world.

Without being perfect parents, and of course by slipping many times from our ideals, my wife and I found a way to raise our children by inspiration. Showing how to be "in spirit" is what the word *inspired* actually means, that is, "to breathe in the breath of God." And such modeling also shows what it means to have enthusiasm, which comes from the Greek words *en theos,* meaning "in God."

This last point is probably the most important. As parents, if you really want to impart spiritual laws to your children in a practical way, you need to know whether you are being successful or not. The easiest way to tell is to see if your children are inspired and enthusiastic. Inspiration, enthusiasm, and delight are spiritual qualities. Without them, there is no spiritual life at any age.

This is an opportunity to express my deep-felt

Parenting and the Gift of Spirit

gratitude to my wife, Rita, whose instinct for love and kindness always led the way for me. Being led by her spiritual instincts also implied those things we *didn't* do as parents. We didn't command obedience or set ourselves up as authorities. We didn't pretend always to know the answers. We didn't suppress our feelings or tell our children that it was good for them to. And we tried every day to raise them to live their own lives, not the lives we regretted not having lived ourselves.

All these practices can be boiled down to one precept: *Every child needs as much mature love as you can give.* What makes love mature—and not just adult—is the conscious spiritual intention behind it. The birth of a baby launches us as teachers of spirit. Afterward we rely on the grace of love, which guides our intentions in the years to come. Spirit lifts us above our individual fallibility, and in doing that it teaches our children the deepest, most valuable lessons.

PART TWO

Practicing the Seven Spiritual Laws

There are two lasting bequests we can hope to give our children. One of these is roots; the other, wings.

HODDING CARTER

Starting when your children are very young, you can integrate the Seven Spiritual Laws into your family routine. If this is done naturally, without forcing or pressure, your children will grow up with living examples of how spirit makes life successful.

A child's understanding of the meaning of the laws will grow with time. Remember that children mainly learn from what you are, not what you say. Your own practice is always the greatest positive influence. Children need you as a model and example; in that sense, watching you is their practice from very early on. If they see you growing and changing and finding more meaning and joy in your own life, the expression "being in harmony with the universe" takes on practical force. They will want that for themselves, even if they don't yet grasp the principles involved.

In the following pages I've outlined a day-by-day program for the family. Each day of the week is devoted to a single law, beginning with Sunday and the Law of Pure Potentiality. In our family we spend some time every day discussing the meaning of a law, and we agree to look for examples of how that law worked for us that day.

In general, all spiritual practice is centered in alertness—just by paying attention to the Seven Spiritual Laws, you invoke their organizing power in your life.

Each day's routine also contains three activities that help to focus your attention on the law for that day. On Sunday the three activities are silent meditation, communion with Nature, and the practice of non-judgment. Everyone in the family, children and parents, agrees to spend a little time on these activities; it is best if this is time shared with the whole family.

Practicing the Seven Spiritual Laws

All in all, these three activities don't take more than a few minutes, at most half an hour. Paying attention isn't a matter of time, anyway, it's a matter of using your awareness. It can take a split second to notice something beautiful. It takes no time at all to stop judging others as right or wrong.

The culmination of each day is dinnertime, when we all talk about what we've done and observed and learned during the day. This discussion is casual and unforced. Whoever wants to speak up does, in as few or as many words as feel comfortable. At the beginning, while the Seven Spiritual Laws are new, you as parents may have to do a little coaxing to encourage your children to comment, but in very short order they will catch on—after all, this is their time to be heard, to have you pay attention to them in a wholly positive way.

Sunday

is the day of Pure Potentiality.

Today we tell our children,
"Everything is possible, no matter what."

On Sunday we agree as parents to do the following things with our children:

1. Lead them in a few minutes of silent meditation

2. Inspire them to appreciate the beauty and wonder of Nature

3. Show them the hidden possibilities in familiar situations

Anyone can count the seeds in an apple;

no one can count the apples in a seed.

ANONYMOUS

On Sunday the family pays attention to the idea that everything is possible. The field where everything is possible is spirit; this is our source. Within everyone is the seed of creativity that can grow in any direction. Nothing limits us except ourselves, for the truest aspect of each person is unbounded potential.

By connecting with our source we activate all possibilities in daily life. In practice this means that we all take time to experience the silent field of pure awareness. Children need to learn that silence is the home of spirit. All other voices speak out loud, but spirit communicates without making a sound.

Being in touch with the field of all possibilities means that you experience self-referral—that is, you look within for guidance. Self-referral brings fulfillment of the spirit that cannot be achieved by material success. The reason we want success is to reach our potential for happiness and wisdom, not just our potential to earn and acquire. Sunday is a good day to ground the whole week on such beliefs.

With children, using the vocabulary of the heart is often more effective than using abstract words like *potentiality.* "Listen to your heart, your heart knows" is a good beginning, along with sentences like these:

> Set your heart on being all you can be.
> In your heart, anything is possible.
> In your heart you know things are going to
>   work out for the best.
> If you're pure of heart, you can bring anything
>   to you.
> No matter what seems to be going on around
>   you, in your heart you'll know that you
>   can do it.

You should also make clear that *heart* isn't just another word for emotions. The heart is a spiritual center. It contains silence and wisdom. Certainly the truest emotions, such as love and compassion, arise from this source, but we want our children to locate the heart as a place where the sense of "I am" resides. This is the seed of inspiration from which all possibilities flow; it is our connection to the field of pure potential. No one is a success who doesn't feel successful in his or her heart of hearts.

Sunday with the Children

The three activities for Sunday are meditating, appreciating Nature's wonder and beauty, and learning to see new possibilities in familiar situations.

1. Adults in the family should practice a period of silent meditation lasting 15–20 minutes in the morning and afternoon. Young children can be nurtured in this practice gradually. From the time your children are the age of six or seven, begin to teach them that a few minutes of being alone and quiet every day is good. Before this age, do not make any attempt to suppress your children's natural energy and enthusiasm.

Inner silence is a delicate experience that cannot blossom until the nervous system has begun to mature. Until your children are age twelve or so, it is enough just to set a personal example. Rather than insist that meditation become part of the daily routine, wait for relaxed opportunities to invite a child to sit still with you (preferably while you are doing your own meditation) and breathe quietly with eyes closed. Ask her to feel the breath as it softly goes in and out; an older child might be asked to visualize the breath as a soft blue-white light going in and out of the nostrils. Say something encouraging. Indicating that you enjoy your own meditation is a good way to provide incentive.

Five minutes of this simple breathing exercise is enough at the outset. Increase to 15 minutes by ages ten to twelve.

Don't be impatient if your child doesn't take to sitting still every time you invite him to. If all you get is fidgeting, just have him go out while you continue your meditation. The example of your own enjoyment will draw your child into the practice naturally.

Practicing the Seven Spiritual Laws

What should your own meditation practice be? I advocate either the breathing meditation just described or Primordial Sound Meditation. (This is taught at The Chopra Center for Well Being as well as by the teachers trained there. You can call the Center in La Jolla, California, to locate a qualified teacher in your area.)

Meditation without knowledge loses half its value, therefore, whatever you can say to your children about the benefits of meditation will be extremely encouraging. Inner silence promotes clarity of mind; it makes us value our inner world; it trains us to go inside to the source of peace and inspiration when we are faced with problems and challenges.

2. Nature breathes the breath of spirit. Its beauty reflects our souls' wonder at being here. So when you take time to go out into a natural setting— walking in the park, hiking a nature trail, picnicking at the beach or in the mountains—infinite creativity can be seen in every tiny flower. I love the saying "What God can give us is limited only by our ability to appreciate His gifts." In terms of success this is

totally true—you can see as far as your vision permits. Nature is the perfect place to stretch your horizon.

Children love to be inspired by natural wonders, and you can support the experience by pointing out how expanded and free Nature makes us feel. The sense of "I can do anything" wells up naturally when you contemplate the vast open sky or the glories of a towering mountain range. People who focus on the physical aspects of Nature tend to dwell on how small and insignificant human beings seem to be on Nature's vast scale, but this isn't true on the spiritual plane. Spiritually, the infinite vistas of the natural world make us feel that we can be at one with infinity.

3. Every second of time is a doorway to unbounded possibilities. Yet if you are not open to them, these possibilities shrink. It's important, therefore, to teach children to reach for something new in a well-known situation. What does it take to see new things? You need insight and perceptiveness, freedom from judgment, a willingness to be open.

Success hinges on all these things, and you will be teaching all of them whenever you pose the simple question "Is there another way of looking at this?"

There always is. For example, a friend of mine was invited to dinner recently. At the doorstep he was told not to mind Claudia, the youngest child in the family, if she didn't eat. "We have problems with her. She's six, and she's just stubborn about not eating," the parents said. When my friend sat down to dinner, Claudia immediately went into her pattern of "I don't like this," "What is it?" and so on—a well-worn routine that the parents greeted with "Nothing can be done about it." In other words, everyone concerned was voicing those thoughts that keep us imprisoned in old, uncreative patterns.

On sheer impulse, my friend leaned over to Claudia and whispered, "That food on your plate looks so good, I want it for myself." He drew a line down the center of her plate with his knife. "Okay, everything on this side of the line is mine, and you can't touch it, no matter what." This was all said in a playful tone.

Claudia looked wide-eyed. She had always faced dinner as a trial, a power struggle with her parents. Now my friend was making it into a game. He looked away and said in a loud voice, "Claudia's not eating my food, is she? She wouldn't do that, would she?"

Of course Claudia couldn't help but eat everything on "his side" of her plate as fast as possible. The temptation to play the game was just too great. This is a good example of how reframing a situation allowed everyone, parents included, to break through old barriers.

Without noticing it, each of us imposes limits on the way we perceive the world. We are faced with infinite, boundless possibilities, yet we don't seize them—or we seize them very rarely—because our past conditioning is always forcing us to pass judgment. Our minds say:

> I don't like it.
> I can't understand it.

> I already know all about it.
> It's wrong (or bad or boring).
> Nothing can be done about it.

This is a good day to catch yourself and your children when you make one of these statements out loud. They happen all the time. Someone or something crosses our path, and we instantly pass judgment, which seals off any flow of new possibilities. Therefore, when you notice even a single instance, shift your perception. Ask your children to look for some new quality in themselves or someone else; ask for a stretch of imagination. Invite fantasy, experimentation, openness.

If you can be the teacher of this thing only, you will do more for your children's success than you could by any other means—success is synonymous with grasping opportunities others have passed by.

Once older children are ready for more abstract concepts, it's extremely valuable to teach non-judgment. Non-judgment means not labeling other people and their ways "right" or "wrong." It is the first step toward the mature attitudes of acceptance, nonviolence, and compassion for life.

Passing judgment is not part of a spiritual person's approach to life. We all project negativity onto other people, but we do this because we confuse our emotional reactions with reality. If people make us angry, distressed, afraid, and so on, we feel that this negativity is their responsibility. Spiritually, the Law of Pure Potentiality tells us that no one can be labeled or judged because life is all possibilities; everything is inside ourselves. Nothing in our nature can be created or destroyed by someone "out there." The very person who makes you angry or afraid can have the opposite effect on someone else. So it is worth setting aside some time on this day to see everyone in the light of love, to hold no judgment, to call no one bad or wrong.

Non-judgment isn't easy to communicate to young children. Even a simple statement like "Don't say your little brother is wrong" becomes confusing, since it can easily be interpreted as a reprimand; any time you use the word *don't* or *stop* or *no,* you are passing your own judgments. It's far better to take a positive approach: ask each child to find one good thing or one lovable thing in another child. Make that the task for the day, and then discuss it at dinner.

In truth none of us should outgrow this simple game, but you can start to ask older children to take responsibility for how they feel. This means that they begin to learn the difference between "You did something that made me mad" and "I have angry feelings I want to deal with myself."

Don't push on this front, however, since it takes a lifetime to grow into mature responsibility for how we feel. Projection is a powerful force. But if you teach acceptance and tolerance, imparting the belief that everyone is doing the best they can and should be seen in that light, not as we expect them to behave, then you will be doing a great deal to teach the First Law.

REFLECTIONS
ON THE LAW OF PURE POTENTIALITY

Everything flows from the infinite source,
which is God. . . .
God is part of every child,
connecting every child with the source.

Since God creates everything,
a child should be encouraged to believe that
everything is possible in his or her life.

Everyone can get in touch
with the seed of God that is inside. . . .
Every day brings a chance to water that seed
and watch it grow.

When children feel small and weak,
remind them that they are children of the universe.

Monday

is the day of Giving.

Today we tell our children, "If you want to get something, give it."

On Monday we agree as parents to do the following things with our children:

1. Invite them to give one thing to someone else in the family

2. Inspire them to receive graciously

3. Share a brief ritual of gratitude for life's gifts

If you would take, you must first give.

LAO-TZU

On this day we pay attention to ways we can give to others. Because there is no giving without receiving, we complete the cycle by paying attention to receiving as well. Giving is thus seen as constant movement, the circulation of everything in creation. Creating anything implies taking some seed or inspiration and giving birth to it. In this giving the seed grows, the fruits multiply, and the inspiration finds form.

Spiritually, success depends on following the laws that govern Nature's workings, and giving is among the most valuable. Many spiritual masters have taught, as the modern yogi Shivananda puts it, that "giving is the secret of abundance." There is no mystery to this; it has always been true that to get love you must first give it, and God always gives all things from love. When we give, we show our understanding of the truth that spirit is the giver of all.

It's not always easy to resist the urge to take and hoard. These tendencies are born from ignorance of spiritual law. Children love to give, and if they start not to give, that is a reflection of the attitudes they see in us. Even a grown-up who constantly says, "Learn to share. Be good and give your little brother some. Be a good girl and you'll get something nice," may still be communicating, at a deeper level, her own gnawing fear of lack and scarcity and the ego's need to possess and hold on. These deep-seated beliefs defeat the spirit of giving. Devoting this day to giving is far more important than what you give in material terms.

Monday with the Children

Except for the very youngest children, Monday is a school day, so we discuss the Law of Giving at breakfast and dinner. At breakfast we set the agenda for the day; at dinner we all share what we've accomplished and learned. The same holds true for all the other laws that fall on weekdays. (But remember, the minutes of silence that are practiced on Sunday get repeated every day, during the times in the morning and afternoon when you do your own meditation.)

The three activities for Monday involve giving to someone else in the family, receiving graciously, and performing a brief ritual of gratitude.

1. Make it a practice as a family to have every member give something to someone else. These gifts should not be elaborately planned or worked over. Remembering to give a smile, a word of encouragement, or help with a chore is natural and simple. It is also what is likely to last, for simple giving within the home cultures the desire to serve. Success is combined with fulfillment when there is an ample aspect of service in it.

Some families find that a big problem can develop over this issue of giving, sharing, and serving. Children naturally want to give. It is unfortunate that people so thoughtlessly repeat the statement "Children are born selfish." Selfishness results from a young child not yet understanding how things actually work. To a very young child, letting go of a toy is the same as losing it permanently; grabbing a piece of candy is a natural response because a young child doesn't yet realize that there is more than one piece, or that the one can be shared.

Observing my own children when they were young, I found that their faces lit up when they had the opportunity to give, and not because they thought they would receive anything in return. We begin to doubt that the universe will return things to us only after our minds get imprinted by fear, lack, abandonment, and greed. Without these imprints, it is obvious that life is a flow of infinite things, some material, some not. How much did anyone have to pay for the air, rain, and sunlight that sustain our life?

People who forget how to give have reverted to a primitive state of consciousness—they believe that if they let go of something, it is gone forever. They forget that we receive anything only because the universe wants us to experience its inner significance for ourselves. In every getting there is a spiritual lesson.

Mere possessions are no substitute for the satisfaction, contentment, and inner fulfillment that are meant to go with them.

You should concentrate with your children on how it *feels* to give. To make sure that the feeling is pleasurable, first treat giving as sharing. Even a three- or four-year-old can feel how nice it is to give a friend one piece of candy if she has two. Older children can be taught to give less tangible things, such as a smile, a kind word, or help to someone in need. Set these as goals for the day and then discuss how things went at dinner.

With children ages twelve and above, the emphasis changes yet again. They are old enough to learn to give when it is not so easy, when one is tempted to withhold or to be selfish. It is at this age that you can talk about how holding on causes pain to the heart and makes others see one as selfish. Learning to give praise to the winner of a game you've just lost, to treat outsiders with kindness and include them in your clique, and to offer help with tact and a lack of self-importance are all appropriate lessons for older children.

2. To receive graciously is an art that cannot be faked. If it is more blessed to give than to receive, it is much harder to receive than to give. We receive ungraciously out of pride, feeling that we don't need anyone's help, handouts, or charity, or out of some sense of discomfort. These are all ego reactions, and there is no need to have them once you realize that the giver is never the giver, just as the receiver is never the receiver. Both stand in for spirit.

Every breath we take is a gift, and in that realization, we see that receiving from another person is a symbol of receiving from God. Every gift is a gesture of love that stands in for divine love, and should be received as such. With younger children, this isn't a problem—they love to receive and have no difficulty lighting up with gratitude.

At later ages the onset of ego needs clouds the issue somewhat. We've all experienced the grudging

Practicing the Seven Spiritual Laws

thank-you forced out of a child's mouth by a parent when no gratitude is present. This attitude can be changed only by having your children continue to pay attention to how it feels to receive. If attention is paid from an early age, the natural warmth and happiness of receiving will not fade. Any person at any age must feel grateful in order to show gratitude. Such feelings can be supported by teaching that all things come from the universal source. Every time we receive, we are given a glimpse of divine love, whoever that love happens to be acting through at the moment.

3. A ritual of gratitude, shared by the whole family, is a nice way to acknowledge the gift of life. You might hold hands at the dinner table and give thanks, not just for the food on the table but for all that has been given that day. Have each family member mention one thing, such as "I'm thankful for the beautiful butterfly I saw on the way home from school," "I'm thankful we're all well and happy," "I give thanks for getting a part in the school play," and so on.

THE SEVEN SPIRITUAL LAWS FOR PARENTS

In many families the ritual of saying blessing has grown stale, and the holiday of Thanksgiving has all but dwindled into meaninglessness. To reverse this takes conscious effort, with the emphasis on *conscious*. It takes awareness to remember that life is a gift, however overwhelmed we may be by other thoughts and pursuits. The joy and enthusiasm you can feel for the spirit reflects back onto you.

Practicing the Seven Spiritual Laws

REFLECTIONS
ON THE LAW OF GIVING

*All good things move around. They don't like to be
locked in one place.*

*In Nature's cycle, giving brings forth receiving, and
receiving brings forth giving.*

*Everyone has already received God's greatest gift—
the potential to grow.*

*When you give, you show your appreciation to the
source of all things.*

We only keep what we give away.

Tuesday

is the day of "Karma."

Today we tell our children, "When you make a choice, you change the future."

On Tuesday we agree as parents to do the following things with our children:

1. Talk about some choice they made today

2. Show them how our future was changed by a past choice we made

3. Explain right and wrong in terms of how choices feel

Certain are the blessings growing out of your good actions.

BUDDHA

Because it is a specialized term, I have put the word "karma" in quotation marks, but any instance of cause and effect falls under this heading. Questions like "Why should I choose this instead of that?" or "What will happen if I approach a problem this way instead of that?" arise every day in children's lives. Children need to know that each choice they make leads to results of a kind that will be good or bad for them—in other words, every choice changes the future.

In crude terms, karma is usually interpreted as bringing rewards for good action and punishment for bad. Parents translate this into a system of rewards and punishment without teaching the really crucial thing: Nature herself handles such matters. A popular cynical saying holds that "life isn't fair," when karmically the exact opposite is true. Life is completely fair. But the workings of life can be deep and hidden, and effects can follow causes on many levels. It is up to us not to judge what result an action deserves but to observe closely how the cause-and-effect universe works, then to model our behavior accordingly.

Here the Seven Spiritual Laws seem to run into conflict with received opinion, for the Law of Karma states that there is no unfairness, no accidents, no victimization—all things are ordered according to an inescapable system of cosmic cause and effect. Karma is not fatalism; it doesn't dictate that people have to suffer. What it does dictate is that free will is absolute. There is no divine power keeping us from making bad choices, nor is there an escape clause that nullifies the universal rule "As you sow, so shall you reap."

Karma, then, involves awareness in several areas: witnessing how choices get made, evaluating their outcome, and listening to your heart, the place where subtle emotional signals indicate when actions are right or wrong. All these strategies can be communicated to children when we teach them how to make choices. Choice in all its complexity is critical to success in life, for success is just a name for the desirable results we wish to achieve through our actions.

Tuesday with the Children

The three activities for Tuesday all center on talking about choices—how we make them, how they change our lives, what results to expect when we favor one way over another.

1.   Talk to each of your children about one choice he or she made today. Naturally the sky's the limit here, because every moment is filled with choices—just encourage anything that comes to their minds. Whatever the choice—making a new friend, spending money on something, deciding not to play with A or B—begin to explore what happens when choices are made. Without setting down hard-and-fast rules (which would kill the spontaneity of

the discussion), you can start to teach your children about the intricate mechanisms of cause and effect, of sowing and reaping.

When a choice is brought up, gently explore it by asking questions such as "How did you feel about that?"; "What do you think will happen?"; "What will you do if that happens instead?" Choice is intimately personal, and as much as you might be tempted to try to control your children's choices of playmates, activities, hobbies, school subjects, and so on, the best way to use your influence is to make your children into sensitive, aware choice makers.

For young children, choice is often crude and indiscriminate. As soon as they learn to talk, toddlers automatically say, "Let me do it," "I want to," and the like. This is an assertion of will, and will drives choice. Only later does a child begin to see that choices lead to consequences. The ego doesn't enjoy not getting its way, and it would be absolute ruler of our lives if negative results didn't arise from actions that are not right for us. Thus karma constantly teaches us to discriminate between what we want and what we know is good for us.

This theme comes up naturally in every child's life. Every child wants more than she gets, and our task is to show our children that choice isn't an endless stream of willful demands. The universe listens to choices from the depth at which they are made. To choose love and truth, for example, is very deep and brings good rewards. To choose selfishness is shallow and brings little reward.

I don't believe it's helpful to use the time-honored statement "Every good deed is its own reward." This implies an inattentive or blind universe. Spiritual masters have all asserted that God or spirit rewards virtue; nothing is left unrewarded, in the sense that no action occurs in a vacuum. Karma is a computing system that gives back what we put in, but with a measure of grace added. If we had omniscient vision at all levels, as God does, we would certainly accept any so-called negative result, because we would see that *nothing better could result*.

The fact that every action leads to the best result possible is a law known as grace. *Grace* is God's loving organization of time and space. It allows us free will to do anything we want, and the results of our actions, whether pleasant or unpleasant, are brought back to us at the perfect time to learn from what we chose. In other words, anything that happens to us reflects a loving guardianship of our well-being.

Children need to learn, then, that pleasure and pain aren't the ultimate guide of whether an action is good or bad for them. By observing how cause and effect work, a child gradually sees that life is a learning process on many levels. Quite often an action can be judged solely on whether it brings pleasure or pain, but many times other factors enter in.

2. It's helpful as children grow older to tell them stories about the choices that affected your life. Instinctively children know that life is a quest; they may have to learn that the future depends on the choices they make, but emotionally they intuit that adults have made many important choices. When

Practicing the Seven Spiritual Laws

you talk about your choices, don't voice them in terms of regrets. "I did this wrong, so I'm going to make sure you never do the same" may be well intended, but your offspring are going to try a little bit of everything. That is inevitable. Besides, a parent's wish is always for the children to have more choices, not fewer, and more choices can be overwhelming unless they are accompanied by the ability to choose.

3. Talk to your children about how it feels to make one choice over another. Childhood is the age when we first decide whether results are more important than emotions. Discussions therefore tend to take a familiar shape: "You won the game when you didn't pick that weak boy to be on your team, but how did you feel when you looked at him? How did he feel?" Or "Your friends asked you to cut school, and now you're afraid they'll think you just suck up. But how would you have felt knowing that you weren't where you should have been?" Or "You didn't pick up your room when I asked you to. Did you have a certain feeling about that?"

The critical factor in being a good choice maker is usually not the rational reason for doing one thing as opposed to another but how each choice felt. This is because, in spiritual terms, intuition is a subtler faculty than reason. Evaluating cause and effect is more emotional than intellectual: our hearts tell us when an action is right or wrong or in some gray zone of doubt.

From an early age you can teach your children to notice if doing something wrong feels bad. Later on, the concept of having a conscience can be introduced, and finally, after age twelve or so, you can begin to discuss the more abstract aspects of how actions and results are intimately linked. I don't mean teaching "you have to pay if you do something wrong"—this implies that we all live under divine threat. There is no divine threat; the only reason that certain negative results seem to come out of the blue is that we are not in touch with the deeper levels of Nature. We violate spiritual law through ignorance.

Because we are a results-oriented society, and one where praise and fame often go to people who've

Practicing the Seven Spiritual Laws

earned their success in ways that are harmful to both themselves and others, the heart value of karma is often overlooked. Yet recently the notion of "emotional intelligence" has come into vogue, and it has been strongly linked to success. Emotional intelligence centers on empathy; it tells us how an action will affect someone else; we feel in advance what they will feel. Choices made on the basis of promoting other people's well-being tend to result in more success than choices made solely out of self-interest. This may be a surprising finding in a materialistic culture, but it is totally predictable through the Law of Karma. Asking your child, "How does that choice feel?" and "How did it make the other person feel?" is primary to both emotional intelligence and good karma.

A critical part of emotional intelligence is learning to delay immediate gratification. Children who learn to be patient, to wait for results rather than grab immediate gain, are much more successful in life than children who must gratify every whim immediately. This is particularly true in relationships, since learning to see beyond one's immediate reactions is the first step toward empathy, and without empathy for another person's feelings, lasting relationships are impossible.

Spiritually, emotional intelligence is connected to the vitally important issue of ego boundaries. If you feel that you are a person isolated in time and space, disconnected from others, there is no reason to obey any guidance except your own impulses. But if you see that your ego is not the real you, that your self extends without limit throughout all of Nature, then you can afford to act in ways that are altruistic, unselfish, and empathetic because you realize, at the deepest level, that "you" and "I" are one. Thus actions are not limited to what "I" want; results are not bound by what happens to "me." There is an overall flow to life that embraces everyone in a larger divine purpose. Teaching children to observe this flow, to see how their lives fit into the universe as a single cell fits into the body, is extremely valuable. The lessons of emotional intelligence can be extended far beyond the emotions to the realm of all action and reaction.

Practicing the Seven Spiritual Laws

In practical terms, what we do on this day is observe our immediate reactions and then ask, "Is this all there is to a situation?" Introduce the notion that every situation contains aspects beyond what any one person can see. How do other people see the situation? For example, how did the loser of a game feel if your child was the winner? How does your child feel when someone else hurts her feelings? Show that it is possible to empathize by putting the shoe on the other foot. Through these gentle instructions on witnessing how things work, you can make karma very real and concrete.

REFLECTIONS
ON THE LAW OF KARMA

No debt goes unpaid in the universe.

Don't grieve over losses—you can only lose what is unreal, and when it is gone, the real will be left behind.

To bring yourself love and happiness, do what you can to bring them to others.

If you don't see an immediate result to good or bad action, be patient and observe.

Wednesday

is the day of Least Effort.

*Today we tell our children, "Don't say no—
go with the flow."*

On Wednesday we agree as parents to do the following things with our children:

1. Find the game in at least one task

2. Reduce the effort it takes to accomplish something important

3. Look for ways Nature has helped us

Cooperate with your destiny,
don't go against it, don't thwart it.
Allow it to fulfill itself.

NISARGADATTA MAHARAJ

The simple phrase "Go with the flow" is actually very significant spiritually. The ancient Greek philosopher Heraclitus declared that life is like a river—you cannot step into it in the same place twice. Existence is always new, yet we are tempted to bring old reactions to it. When we find ourselves resisting anything—which basically means saying no—we are usually trying to impose an old belief or habit on a new situation.

The Law of Least Effort bids us to recognize the newness of life by allowing it to unfold without interference. It tells us to be in the moment, to look for Nature's help, and to stop blaming anyone or anything outside ourselves. In the flow, spirit is already organizing the millions upon millions of details that uphold life—from the infinite processes needed to keep a single cell alive to the vast intricacies of the evolving universe. By connecting with spirit, we ride this cosmic organizing power and take advantage of it.

For many adults, however, the concept of least effort is a difficult one. Our technology is constantly trying to find ways to save work through more efficient machines, but translating this to the human level is not easy. The biggest obstacle is our work ethic, which holds that more work reaps greater rewards. There are two flaws in this. First, Nature herself operates through least effort—the laws of physics dictate that any process, from the spin of an electron to the spin of a galaxy, must function according to the most efficient expenditure of energy, with the least drag. Second, human advancement always comes through ideas, inspiration, and desire. These occur spontaneously; there is no amount of work that can force inspiration, or desire, or even consistently good ideas.

If going with the flow is hard for us, it comes very naturally to a child. Hardly any instruction is needed before age six or so, since young children

immediately take the course of least resistance—
they reach for what they want, say what they have to
say, express the emotion that rises with the moment.
And their chief activity is not work but play. We can
introduce older children to the interrelated ideas of
not resisting, putting up no defense, and taking
responsibility for how one chooses to work. *Acceptance* is essential because a lot of effort is wasted
whenever you put up resistance. Defenselessness is
tied to acceptance, in that having to defend your
point of view creates conflict and chaos, which are
both huge wastes of energy.

Trying to get our own way is a temptation few of
us can resist, but the Law of Least Effort tells us that
we can have our way through means other than struggle and conflict. We can follow the flow of spirit,
knowing that its infinite organizing power will tend
to our wants. Thus the Law of Least Effort brings in
faith and patience. We were all taught that fighting
and struggle are the route to success. In reality, it is
much more important to have faith in your own
desires. When you assume that other people exist to
block you from achieving what you want, you have
no choice but to constantly defend yourself. Teach-

ing a child that there is a wish-granting power far beyond the power of other people is a valuable lesson.

The third element in the Law of Least Effort is responsibility. Children should also be taught that success and fulfillment come from inside, and it is only inside that matters. Each of us is responsible for how we feel, what we wish for, and how we decide to approach life's challenges. The highest responsibility is fulfilled not by doing a huge amount of work but by doing the work of spirit in an attitude of joy and creativity. This is the only way that life without struggle becomes possible.

Wednesday with the Children

The three activities for Wednesday are finding the game in a task, reducing work, and looking for ways Nature helps us.

1. The ancient Vedic scriptures of India say that the whole cosmos is a *lila,* or play of the gods—

Practicing the Seven Spiritual Laws

meaning that this is a recreational universe. By finding the game in even one task today, you teach your
children the divine way to approach work. Most of
the time, you as parents can make a task into a game
by removing the pressures that obstruct play. These
include warnings, threats, time pressures, guilt
tripping, and offers of money or other rewards for
work done.

Despite your own ingrained work ethic, there are
certain spiritual truths concerning work:

> Spirit doesn't blame for work not done.
> Life doesn't depend on whether something
>   gets done or not.
> Work isn't the source of happiness.
> Your attitude toward your work, not the task
>   itself, comes first.

Thus a task that waits to get done until you feel
relaxed and comfortable about it is a task well done.
The exact opposite of this attitude is perfectionism.
Perfectionism is rooted in fear and control. It masks

the hidden feeling "I won't survive if I don't do this exactly as God wants it," implying that God is a blaming, unloving taskmaster.

In reality God wants you to enjoy this recreational universe, and the sooner you teach your children that doing so is all right, the more chance you give them to be successful. By definition successful people enjoy what they do. They have found the only way to be in "the zone" or "the flow," which is to relax. Relaxation is the prerequisite for that inner expansion that allows a person to express the source of inspiration and joy within.

Having realized this, set an example for your children by turning any task—vacuuming the rug, picking up their room, mowing the lawn—into a game or a source of stimulation. You can practice a song while taking out the garbage or make up a poem washing the dishes.

Games take a little more invention: "We're not just going to vacuum today, we're looking for ghosts.

Didn't you know that ghosts run away from vacuum cleaners? They can't stand them." With this as a start, have one of your children be the ghost. After the "ghost" hides, the child with the vacuum goes into the designated room and tries to lure the ghost out by vacuuming under the bed, in the closet, behind the sofa, etc. Once you find the ghost, you get to trade places and become the ghost in the next room. (If you have only one child, cut out a paper ghost and hide it somewhere to be found, or five ghosts, and give a prize if more than four are found.)

Making up games is a good way to reverse our own tendency to forget that life is meant to be approached as play, reflecting the divine play of the cosmos. The maturing process can be a numbing, even deadening process. To combat this tendency, find the game in your own activities, the joy as the heart of work. Show your own enjoyment to your children, and as soon as any task isn't fun or the game grows stale, stop working. There's no harm in a job well done, but a job done in an attitude of fatigue, struggle, and imposition isn't worth doing.

The results of your work will be clouded by the negativity that comes with them.

2. Set aside a few minutes for the whole family to concentrate on reducing effort, strain, and wear and tear. Talk at the dinner table about times when solutions appeared that were much easier than you thought they would be. The whole drift is to defuse the notion, which bombards us from every side, that life is a problem. In spiritual terms, life is not problematic; only our attitudes toward it are. Your children are going to hear from dozens of people a day that things are hard, tough, difficult, a struggle, even overwhelming. (If you think this isn't happening among grade-school children, just listen to interviews with third- and fourth-graders complaining about the pressure to achieve that is already crippling their chance for happiness and forcing them to cope with stress at inconceivably early ages.)

Reducing the amount of work in a situation sometimes calls for a mechanical solution, such as using a more powerful computer to solve a technical prob-

Practicing the Seven Spiritual Laws

lem, but more often what's needed is a shift in attitude. Nothing is more efficient than spirit. When you can invoke spirit, you have more chance for success than under any other circumstance. Spirit is creative fullness; that is why the Latin word *genius* also means "spirit."

In practice, invoking spirit means the following:

- Being in a good mood for work.
- Approaching tasks with relaxed confidence.
- Not straining or putting excessive demands on yourself physically (e.g., staying up late, working overtime, not taking breaks, not eating and getting enough fluids).
- Meditating regularly.
- Asking for inspiration; being patient until it comes.
- Not resisting changes in the situation.
- Not having to have your own way.
- Not assuming that you know the answer in advance.

Review these points at dinner to reinforce the habits you want your children to develop.

3. When spirit, or Nature, does come to help with a task, its arrival is often silent and unnoticed. Therefore it's good to start children noticing as soon as possible. "Did you get a new idea today?"; "Were you surprised by how easy something that you thought would be hard turned out to be?" You can begin with questions like these and then offer your own examples. The emphasis should be on creative solutions, however trivial seeming, that made you feel inspired. Encouraging such an attitude from the earliest age opens the way for inspiration in years to come.

Practicing the Seven Spiritual Laws

REFLECTIONS
ON THE LAW OF LEAST EFFORT

*Put every effort into organizing your life, but remember
that the ultimate organizer is Nature.*

Don't try to steer the river.

*When Nature is most productive and creative, it does
not work . . . it plays.*

The best work flows from us effortlessly.

Putting up resistance to life ultimately never succeeds.

Allow the gifts of spirit to come to you.

Thursday

is the day of Intention and Desire.

Today we tell our children, "Every time you wish or want, you plant a seed."

On Thursday we agree as parents to do the following things with our children:

1. List clearly all our desires for the week

2. Release our desires for Nature to fulfill

3. Be alert in the present moment, where all fulfillment occurs

Be very careful what you set your heart upon, for you will surely have it.

RALPH WALDO EMERSON

Making our desires come true is at the heart of success, and, for all of us, how we learned to do that dates from childhood. Desire is a tangled issue. It raises hidden questions about how much we deserve, how good we really are, whether God wants us to succeed, and so on. There are so many questions, in fact, that no parent can answer all of them in advance. Success and failure are extremely personal experiences, being intimately linked to who you think you really are deep down.

As parents we therefore want to lay the strongest foundation of self-esteem for the countless experiences of success and failure that will come as our children grow up. Spiritually, desire is never a negative; we were born as creatures of desire. Without it, we would not want to grow. Other creatures don't have to want to grow, because for them the process is genetic; for humans, however, wanting to grow leads the mind toward the source of infinite love, peace, and power that is the very goal of life.

Children need to learn that desire is the path to God, and intention is the chief tool on that path. What you intend for yourself determines what you get. Although it seems like a paradox, you must have a vision of the future in order for the future to surprise you, for without visions, life dwindles into ritual and repetition. A future that merely repeats the present can never be surprising.

The spiritual process that makes desires come true doesn't occur to us as spontaneously as desire itself. It needs to be taught. Lack of success in life is principally due to mental confusion. We fail to notice how deeply conflicted our desires are, for example, causing us to send unwitting mixed messages to the universe. A chronic failure who wishes for wealth, for example, while also wanting to accept no responsibility for himself is in essence sending a contrary input to the cosmic computer, and usually the person cannot see this. Two contrary desires coexist: "I want wealth" and "I don't want to see my situation honestly." Lack of awareness then shifts the blame for failure onto some outside person or circumstance when in reality Nature is giving a response to each wish. It just happens that the wishes are weak, unfocused, and in contradiction with each other.

Being aware of what you want is such an obvious first step in the process of desiring that it is amazing how many people ignore it. Your children have many levels of desire they may not be aware of, just as adults do. Desires don't always arise clearly, and they rarely arise by themselves; they are liberally mixed with fantasy, dreaming, wishing, and projection. Also, desiring is a process that comes in continuous waves, one overlapping the other. We are all working on big desires that take months and years to be fulfilled, along with smaller desires that take days, hours, or minutes.

The more specific your children learn to be with their intentions, the more easily they will be able to order their lives, since order begins in the mind.

Thursday with the Children

The three activities for Thursday center on clarifying the mechanics of desire: listing or stating the desire as specifically as possible, releasing the desire to the universe, trusting in the mechanics of creation to bring you a result, and remaining alert to the present moment, which is where all results occur.

1.   Today have everyone in the family make a list of desires for the coming week and post it on the refrigerator. (You can begin this activity when a child is nine or ten; younger children would just interpret it as making out a list for Santa Claus, since they can't yet grasp the mechanics of intention.)

In guiding your children's lists, ask prompting questions such as "What do you most wish for yourself this week?"; "What do you most wish for someone else?"; "What do you want to happen at school?" Try to avoid the tendency for the list to simply become a series of acquisitions—i.e., a new bicycle or a computer game.

Point out instead that the universe is always bringing to us a stream of results and rewards that stem from our wishes and wants. Wishes and wants are like seeds, and the things that happen to us are the sprouting of those seeds. Some seeds take a long time to sprout—a child inspired to play the piano can be planting a seed that grows for a lifetime, for example. All of us are working on both big and small desires. Not all of these can come true at once. Each desire has its own season, its own way of coming true.

Encourage your children to want happiness and fulfillment, the absence of conflict and struggle, and other spiritual rewards as primary desires. But also encourage the sprouting of seeds that you see as valuable on any level—a budding talent, a good tendency at school or in personal relationships, being less shy or better at a certain game or subject, for instance.

And what about younger children who aren't ready to make lists or think about desires as intentions? Try a more concrete approach: actually plant a bean seed between two wet blotters and show them the miracle of germination. Then transplant the seed and tell them that if they want the seedling to grow, they need to help water it and care for it. The metaphor of the seed is applicable at every age, since it relates directly to the mechanics of Nature.

2. Releasing your desire is not the easiest thing for children to grasp, especially if they have developed the habit of seeing their parents as the source of all the things they want. Many parents, faced with children who unendingly try to wheedle things out of them, would be horrified at the thought of teaching them to want more. The point is to want *more efficiently*. Releasing a desire to the universe is part of being efficient, because making wishes and wants come true is never solely in anyone's power.

Success comes from any and all directions.

Once you realize this, you can teach your children the principle of patient expectation. That is, once you know what you want, you stay relaxed about it.

Practicing the Seven Spiritual Laws

The shallow, trivial desires will simply fall away, but those that are sincere and deep will be nourished by Nature. Tell your children that desires kept in the heart come true faster than those we constantly broadcast by talking about them or putting demands on others.

3. At any moment of the day, some desire is in the process of coming true. Old seeds we planted (and perhaps forgot about) are bringing results, mixed in with the beginnings of larger results to come. The point is to make your children aware that the universe (or spirit or God) is always listening; none of us is alone. We are constantly being heeded.

A simple way to remain alert for the universe's response is to keep tabs on the lists you have put on the refrigerator. Ask your children to report on how each desire is coming true throughout the week. You can ask a prompting question like "Did anything really nice happen to you today?" and then point out how the answer fits in with the child's list for that week.

Alertness in the present moment is the fertilizer that keeps fulfillment of desire growing.

Most desires are fulfilled in many small stages, not all at once; this is especially true of the seeds that, once planted, grow for years and years. Every step of fulfillment comes in its own time, at its own moment. Therefore, by being alert to every moment, we receive the results of our wishes. A simple example is happiness. Everyone wants to be happy, but many people expect some epiphany or sudden burst of joy that will last forever. True happiness is not like that; it is a state of well-being that you must be alert to. Otherwise the moment will pass without notice or else be masked by the things outside yourself that seem to be making you happy (or unhappy). Thus remaining alert to the present moment happens inside; to keep looking outside yourself for desires to come true is to miss the real focus of fulfillment.

Many younger children do not have the attention span to follow a desire from inception to completion, but they can still be taught that wanting some-

Practicing the Seven Spiritual Laws

thing doesn't have to lead to demands, whining, and general distress if the fulfillment doesn't come immediately. Being attentive to your children's wants, you stand in for Nature at this early stage. By trusting that you hear what they want, by feeling secure that you want to fulfill their needs, young children make a good start for trusting Nature later on.

Older children are capable of closer and longer observation. They can be taught that desire is a mechanism rooted in the heart, that it doesn't have to be chased in the outside world. The road of our desires is natural—we are led to work for things that bring the deepest fulfillment, that fall in line with our talents and abilities. Desire thus becomes its own teacher, showing a child how to follow inner guidance.

"Is this what you really want?" is an appropriate question to begin to ask children in late grade school, and it remains relevant for life. If the answer is yes, then a child needs to learn that her wish is enough to satisfy God; divine intention aligns with human intention when a desire is pure, focused, and in the best interests of one's spiritual growth. Desires that fail to come true lack one of these ingredients or simply need time.

Practicing the Seven Spiritual Laws

REFLECTIONS
ON THE LAW OF
INTENTION AND DESIRE

Honor the good things you want for yourself, since desire is the path to God.

Every event that baffles you today had its seed in an intention yesterday.

Spirit cannot fulfill any desire until you release it.

As specific, clear, and pure as your intention is, just that clear will be the result brought back to you.

Friday

is the day of Detachment.

Today we tell our children, "Enjoy the journey."

On Friday we agree as parents to do the following things with our children:

1. Talk about the "real you"

2. Show them that uncertainty can be good—no one has to have all the answers

3. Teach them to feel balanced about loss and gain

All life is an experiment. The more experiments you make the better.

RALPH WALDO EMERSON

Enjoy the journey" is a positive expression for an idea that isn't popular in our society. Words have different values in different cultures, and there is no better example than the word *detachment*. For thousands of years, particularly in the East, *detachment* has been a positive word, connoting the ability to find happiness beyond the play of pleasure and pain. In the West, however, our intense fixation on achieving material goals has made *detachment* a negative word, associated with indifference, apathy, and noninvolvement.

There is no doubt that the Eastern attitude can degenerate into fatalism and lack of initiative, but in its pure meaning, detachment implies intense involvement and creativity, albeit with surrender of the outcome. Both are necessary for happiness: passionate involvement gives us the happiness of using our creativity; surrender recognizes that all outcomes depend upon the universe, not on our bounded ego-selves. A wise man is detached from the drama of the material world because he focuses instead on the source from which all dualities of light and darkness, good and evil, pleasure and pain actually originate.

Because it runs so counter to our cultural bias, detachment is not the easiest principle to teach. We can begin with what detachment isn't.

> It isn't detached to say that you don't care.
> It isn't detached to say something isn't your
>   responsibility when it is.
> It isn't detached to ignore the needs and
>   feelings of others.
> It isn't detached to constantly look out only
>   for number one.

Teaching your children to avoid these things is a good way to begin them on the road to detachment. Most of the time, we are tempted to be attached to something, a condition always labeled with "me" or "mine." Holding on to my things, my job, my opinions, my pride, and so forth is the result of fear. We fear that the universe is cold and indifferent, therefore we contract all our energies around this "me" that is supposed to protect us.

Ego contraction, however, prevents precisely the free expansion that enables us to find our connection to spirit. This is often described as the difference between the self and the Self. The self is the isolated ego clinging to its small reality; the Self is the unbounded spirit that can afford not to cling at all.

Detachment means that you live from the Self instead of the self.

Childhood is the critical time for learning about the Self, for this is the period when the ego, and all its needs and fears, starts to develop. When a child simply succumbs to ego, the whole illusion of "I, me, mine" takes hold, and it will be both painful and difficult to break away from in adulthood. Ego has to be tempered with the notion that "I" doesn't have to be ego; I-ness can be a sense of oneness with the field of all possibilities—this has been called cosmic ego. Thus in teaching detachment, you are inviting your children to join you in the cosmic dance.

Detachment is the perspective that allows us to enjoy the journey of life. Such enjoyment is critical to success.

It would also be good to say a little more about the concept of "detached involvement"—throwing yourself with complete enthusiasm into anything you do, but without expecting to control the outcome. Your responsibility is restricted to the actions you undertake; the outcome is left in the hands of spirit. For young children, this concept is not really applicable, because it contains a seeming paradox. How can a person be fully involved and detached at the same time?

The answer can only lie in the field of Being. If you see yourself as identified with spirit, then your individual actions fall into a larger pattern. Being infinite, this larger pattern—we can call it God's divine plan—is beyond any person's rational conception. Detachment is how we show that we leave the larger plan to God; involvement is how we show that we want to participate, since nothing can inspire more passion than to be a co-creator with God.

The wisdom of uncertainty is a closely related concept. Uncertainty is fearful to the ego, which always wants to control reality, but from the viewpoint of detachment, a constantly shifting and changing universe must remain uncertain. If things were certain, there could be no creativity. Therefore spirit works through surprises and unexpected outcomes. The divine love of uncertainty at first seems to contradict the Law of Karma, which says that everything follows cause and effect. But karma isn't the ultimate reality; it is just the mechanics of how things work in the relative world. The ultimate reality is the unfolding of divine creativity. The universe is ultimately a recreational universe; it exists for divine play. The more we realize this, the more we can join the play and be free from all anxiety about how things will turn out. We achieve peace of mind only when we accept the wisdom of uncertainty.

If the universe is uncertain—as Heisenberg's famous principle assures us—then everything is possible. We may feel emotionally comfortable with fixed outcomes, but total fixity would be death. In spiritual terms death is not extinction, it is frozen life, energy that has been forced to stay in one place instead of flowing to its next purpose in God's plan. A complete vision of life must include the realization that anything and everything is destined to happen, and our role is to remain open to uncertainty and surprise.

Friday with the Children

The three activities for Friday involve seeing the world in a more detached way: realizing that the "real you" is spiritual, accepting that uncertainty is inevitable and not to be feared, and being balanced about loss and gain.

These lessons are just a beginning—detachment grows on all levels as spiritual life ripens. Altruism and compassion are the natural results of being detached, as is service to others. Replacing pride with humility is a fruit of detachment; so is the condition Christ called "being in the world but not of it." My favorite expression for detachment is that it makes one a citizen of the universe. All these things are implied in the simple lessons for today.

1. The "real you" is a fascinating topic at any age. Children already feel an age-old attraction to the otherworldly. Stories of God, heaven, and angels are told to children almost from the cradle; fairy tales create a similar world that children accept as imaginary and yet more real than the world around them. With this in mind, you can talk to your children about the Self in understandable ways.

Here's the kind of fable, for example, suitable to tell younger children: "Everyone has an invisible friend who looks after everything they do. You have this friend, and so do your brothers and sisters, and so do Mommy and Daddy. God sent you your friend. Your friend isn't in heaven like the angels but right here, in your heart. You know what your friend's name is? Just the same as your name, because your friend is really part of you. When you love your toys or me or anything else, your friend helps you to feel that love. So you always want to make sure you pay attention whenever you feel sad or angry. Shut your eyes and ask your friend to remind you that we all love you very much, so you must always love yourself. That's what your invisible friend is here to tell you, always."

The Self is a person's soul, which looks down on all events in this world with perfect peace and joy. It is one's connection to God and heaven (if you choose to use those terms) or to the field of all possibilities. Your Self is never hurt or confused; it always loves you; it is always near. Children will be reassured to hear these things, even though it will be a long time before they believe them completely.

To identify fully with the Self requires long experience in meditation, since it is out of the silence of inner awareness that the Self is known. Gradually you begin to realize that this Self isn't just inside you; it permeates all of existence. The infinite complexity of life isn't graspable by the small self—as desperately as one might try to believe otherwise, reality isn't under ego control. The Self organizes reality by observing, allowing, accepting, and ulti-

Practicing the Seven Spiritual Laws

mately joining itself with the cosmic intelligence that organizes all of reality down to the smallest detail.

2.   There is always a delicate balance between giving children security and teaching them that reality can be very insecure. This is a dilemma all parents face, and they usually face it anxiously, afraid that they will err on one side or the other, either instilling false security in their children or going too far in warning them about danger and risk.

Spiritually we have to reconcile these opposing values to feel safe in a shifting, unpredictable world. Uncertainty can't be wished away; therefore it's deeply valuable to come to terms with it, to realize that there is wisdom in uncertainty—the wisdom of a Creator who wants to keep reality fresh, new, and ever-moving toward fulfillment.

How do we communicate this to a child? Young children love surprises, and this is the day to fully indulge your delight in surprising them. Unexpected treats bring joy to giver and receiver, and they need to have no better reason than "I just wanted to do something different"—after all, that's the only reason God needs.

At older ages, uncertainty can seem to be a problem, since it implies a shifting world that is difficult to cope with. Teaching your children to let go and enjoy change as it comes is important, as is direct confrontation of hidden anxiety. With children of five and older, asking if something new is a source of fear is appropriate. All you need is a simple opening like "I know you haven't done this before. Is it a little scary?"

On this day you can also remind yourself not to act in front of the children as if you know everything, as if being an adult means that all questions are settled. This is a sensitive matter, because children are reassured by authority. So you need to put your uncertainty in positive terms. Instead of saying, "I don't have an answer," emphasize that there are a lot of answers and the fun of life is finding out how much you have yet to learn, no matter how much you already know.

3. No one likes to lose things, on any level. Children are as distressed by the death of a pet or the loss of a toy as adults are by the death of a close friend or the loss of a job. Our grief over loss comes from expectation; we expect that having something will make us happier while not having it will make us unhappier. Despite countless cautionary tales that riches don't buy happiness, all of us still equate money and possessions with well-being.

You can begin early to teach your children another way, to look inside rather than to outside things for happiness. This is where the lesson of loss and gain comes in. Treating loss on the material plane alone isn't satisfying to a child. To say, "Don't cry, I'll buy you another doll," is just as shortsighted as to say the opposite, "It's your fault for losing it, you're not getting another."

Both statements assume that the doll is the source of happiness. You are going to have to decide whether or not to replace something that's been lost, but the larger issue is that the doll doesn't matter. Make children feel secure and loved no matter what anyone has or doesn't have. Thus loss can be a reason to reinforce the notion that "the real you" is all right no matter what. Allow the grieving over loss to occur— you shouldn't stand in the way of emotional expression—but put it in perspective: "I know you feel bad now, but it's only a thing, and you are here for much more important reasons than the things you own or don't own."

What are these reasons? In difficult situations, after the emotion has come and gone, you might say something like:

> "You are here to be special, because you are special."
>
> "You are here to find out all kinds of things."
>
> "You are here for Mommy and Daddy to love you and take care of you."
>
> "You are here to make yourself happy in all kinds of ways."

Each statement touches on the notion that "I" am unique, creative, loved, not harmed by loss. Crying over a lost doll isn't the same as losing part of yourself—but you'd be surprised how many children don't realize this simple truth because their parents fail to remind them of it.

In this way the whole matter of loss and gain gets treated at the same time. Countless people grow up thinking that their problems will be solved as soon as they have enough of something—money, fame, status, et cetera. But loss and gain always come in cycles. Ultimately this holds true for life and death, which are forever pursuing each other in the cycle of birth and rebirth.

Detachment is the quality that enables a person to feel unmoved by either loss or gain. Neither affects the Self; the Self is always full. It always gets enough love and happiness from its source to satisfy it. Teach this to your children, constantly focusing on the fact that this same source of love and happiness is always available. The spiritual journey is an unfolding of how much more secure the Self is than the self.

THE SEVEN SPIRITUAL LAWS FOR PARENTS

REFLECTIONS
ON THE LAW OF DETACHMENT

*Detachment means being passionate about your work
but dispassionate about its rewards.*

*Any name or label you identify yourself with is false—
the real you is unbounded and nameless,
beyond all labels.*

*Trusting in yourself, not what you accomplish, is the
key to success.*

*Put yourself in the hands of the universe—then you
will have no need for control.*

*Self-acceptance leads to success, not the
other way around.*

Saturday

is the day of "Dharma."

Today we tell our children, "You are here for a reason."

On Saturday we agree as parents to do the following things with our children:

1. Ask each one, "Where are you right now?"

2. Encourage their unique talents and abilities

3. Invite them to perform an act of service

Everyone's life is a fairy tale written by God's fingers.

HANS CHRISTIAN ANDERSEN

Dharma is a Sanskrit word meaning several things: duty, purpose, and law. In a sense the day of dharma is the day of law, the fulfillment of a whole week devoted to spiritual laws. On this day we reflect on how well we have followed spiritual law, how attuned our existence actually is to the harmony of the universe.

Today we remind our children, "You are here for a reason." Spiritual law is here to serve us as we serve it. It serves us by showing that lasting happiness and fulfillment are possible, indeed inevitable. There is a hidden purpose working for our evolution in every event, every action, every thought. The highest goal in life is to find this purpose and live by it.

On this day we measure our success according

to how fulfilled the week has been, how much ease and opportunity it has brought, what new inspirations and insights have come our way. Then we reflect these things onto our children. The belief that life is unfair seems valid only because we experience the unloving behavior of others, who cannot always share the high levels of consciousness that spirit is trying to inspire.

Purpose is activated only when you have receptivity. Awareness is the key to achieving what the universe has planned for you.

In the family you can reinforce that life is always fair. The dharma ensures this through the force of spiritual law. To say that life is unfair is to imply that it is random, meaningless, capricious, and dangerous. In other words, that it is without spiritual law. So on this day you can counter all such impressions by showing how fair life really is, and what makes it fair is that we are allowed free will to express ourselves with every ounce of creative power at our disposal.

Saturday with the Children

The three activities for Saturday center on life's purpose as it is unfolding for a child. Ask your children, "Where are you right now?," encourage each child's uniqueness, and invite your children to perform an act of service.

1.   The question "Where are you?" is your way of exploring your children's own ideas of their purpose and progress. One's dharma is one's path, which translates into several components:

- Where I think I'm going. This is my vision.
- How I plan to get there. This is my work on the path.
- How far I think I've gotten. This is my level of awareness.
- What I think is holding me back. This is my present challenge or lesson.

To be complete, dharma must contain all these ingredients. A vision without a means of traveling

the path is only a fantasy. Hard work and achievement without a vision are talent being emptied into
the sand. Not all these ingredients need to be ver-
balized every day; a vision, for example, is usually
strongest at the outset, giving place to the work and
obstacles that arise in order to make the vision real.

Even so, it's good to have your children learn to be
aware of their paths. The youngest children have an
instinctive purpose, being happy. But as soon as a
child is old enough to set goals—after age five or
six—measuring progress toward a goal is a necessity.
"Where are you? How are things going? Are you getting close to what you want to achieve? If not, why
not?" With these questions in mind, parents can
begin to encourage each child to feel an intimate
connection with life's purpose day in and day out.

You can also broaden this topic by asking, "Where
are we as a family?" Many families would cringe from
asking such a question, because they do not have
enough openness and intimacy and trust for answers
to come out honestly. Or the parents are too
attached to seeming to have all the answers.

Practicing the Seven Spiritual Laws

From an early age you need to teach your children that expressing how they feel about family matters is all right. The same holds for saying honestly if their personal wishes aren't coming true. Many desires don't come true, at least not immediately; disappointment, discouragement, and frustration are spiritual realities that children do not need to hide from. No path is without its obstacles, and although an obstacle may feel negative on the emotional level, the Law of "Dharma" tells us that some good is hidden within every block. Dharma is universal law; it upholds us in where we need to be. So the ultimate answer to the question "Where are you right now?" is "Just where I need to be."

To give that answer implies great security, and it is this security you want to reinforce with your children. As individuals, we lack the vision to see around every corner in the road; it is not in Nature's way to open up the complete vista, given that surprise and uncertainty are built into the divine plan.

Of course, children are easily frustrated when things don't go exactly right, and it is a lifelong process to become patient and make peace with the notion that every person is just where she needs to be.

2. Making a child feel unique means making him or her feel uniquely *wanted*. Having a talent is one thing; feeling that the universe welcomes it is another. Uniqueness without love is barren and very little different from loneliness. Today you can sit down and list each child's talents, having your children participate, in order to reinforce the notion that talents are given to us by spirit for our happiness and fulfillment.

3. Invite each child to do something kind for someone else, however small the gesture might be. Picking up litter seen while taking a hike, opening a door for an older person, helping younger siblings pick up their room—these are as valuable as charity work. The inner meaning of the gesture is what you want to teach. Helping someone else feels good in a way that just doing something for yourself doesn't— this is the kernel of what you want to impart, not just that service is virtuous or makes a person look

good to others (which is too often the motive for adults).

Serving others fits nicely with the notion that uniqueness is everywhere. When you serve others, you have an opportunity to appreciate their worth; service expresses this appreciation directly. Having a child do nice things for a younger brother or sister or friend leads directly to a sense of how special that friend, brother, or sister is. In this way specialness gets accepted as a quality everyone has.

When you serve others, you remind yourself of your duty as a loving child of the Almighty. *Duty* is a synonym for *dharma,* and the word covers duty to society, duty to oneself, and duty to God. Your duty to society is to serve others; your duty to yourself is to unfold spiritually; your duty to God is to participate in the divine plan for humankind's higher evolution.

As parents, we are not teaching our children hard-and-fast rules that must be heeded. We are inviting them into our own journey, into our sense of pur-

THE SEVEN SPIRITUAL LAWS FOR PARENTS

pose, which never ends. It is a journey of ever-expanding meaning. Although very young children may not be able to understand what this means in words, your child can easily sense whether you find life exciting and wondrous. Your sense of purpose in the universe speaks far louder than any words.

Practicing the Seven Spiritual Laws

REFLECTIONS
ON THE LAW OF "DHARMA"

A life of purpose reveals the purpose of life.

You can never be wrong about destiny. Whether you succeed or not, you are proven to be right.

The universe has a purpose—the fulfillment of human creativity and happiness.

Don't judge your life. Every life is a step toward unity with God.

Don't struggle to find out why you are here— just look closer.

Conclusion

The One Thing
You Cannot Do Without

As a parent, what is the one thing you cannot do without? Most people would automatically say "love," which is certainly right. But then you have to ask a deeper question, "Where does love come from?" By itself, the bond of love isn't enough, because it frays and sometimes breaks. We all raise our children according to what we call love; yet today's young people still have horrendous problems.

Deeper than love, the one thing you can't do without is *innocence*. Innocence is the source of love. Innocence, as I am defining it here, isn't naïveté. Quite the opposite. Innocence is openness. It is based on a deep spiritual knowledge of several critical issues.

Conclusion

Innocence is the knowledge that you can guide children but never control them. You must be open to the person within every child, a person who is bound to be different from you. In innocence, this fact can be accepted with a peaceful heart.

Innocence is the knowledge that life is never certain. Your children are guaranteed to go in directions you cannot predict, to do things you would never do. Uncertainty is a given, because life is nothing but change. In innocence you can accept this—you will let go of your need to make your children conform to your preconceived notions.

Innocence is the knowledge that love is deeper than surface events. On the surface, a child's journey is wayward and difficult. We all want to teach our children those lessons we found were the hardest to learn; we want to protect them from unnecessary pain. But in innocence we realize that the surface of life is a distraction from the deeper journey every person must make. This is the journey of soul-making. Soul-making happens under the watchful eye of spirit. We can help our children realize the essential importance of their souls, but we aren't responsible for the journey. That is a unique agreement made between every person and his or her higher Self.

If I were to take all these points and put them into a single sentence, this would be it: *Innocence is the knowledge that your child is yours and yet not yours.* Everyone is ultimately a child of spirit. We all grew up belonging to a family, but this is a very loose kind of belonging. Mostly we belong to ourselves, which means to our spirit or soul or essence.

Thus to see a child with real love means to see this spark of the divine. It's easy to say that every child is unique and precious, but what really makes it true is innocence, being able to look at a child as a soul embarked on the journey of soul-making. This means giving up some deeply imprinted patterns about parenting.

Parents are used to being authority figures. As such, we are above and beyond our children— smarter, more powerful, more experienced, in command of money and property. From this position of authority, parents have been able to pass judgment, to inflict punishment, to lay down the rules of right and wrong, and to do so with a clear sense of duty and purpose.

This book has outlined a different duty and purpose. In this new vision, a parent isn't an authority. You and your child are both souls; you are both embarked on the journey of soul-making. The only difference is the roles you have chosen. All souls are immortal; they cannot be created or destroyed. But we do choose temporary roles to play.

The most good you can do for yourself spiritually is to play your role as parent with total love, conviction, and purpose. The reason you undertook the role of parent was ultimately selfish—in the best spiritual sense. This is the role that will uplift and inspire you more than any other. The same is true for your child. As an all-knowing, immortal spirit, your child has decided to be a weak, vulnerable infant, totally dependent upon your help. That is the role a child plays, with total conviction and dedication. And yet both of you, if you strip away the role playing, are pure souls, equal and as one. Innocence enables you to see this, to play the role yet go beyond it.

Some people may argue against this whole

Conclusion

notion, but I think every parent has had moments when the look in a child's eye told a tale of infinite wisdom, of experiences that go far beyond this particular moment in time and space. I know this has been true with my own children. I've put them to bed, read stories to them, thrown a ball around with them, and sat proudly through dance recitals. The whole time I was doing this, I was the daddy and they were the kids.

But there have been other, rarer moments when the whole facade fell away. I've seen my son give me a glance that said, "Here we are again. What an interesting game we're playing this time." I've seen my daughter smile in such a way that I just knew she was on the verge of laughing out loud at the masks we have put on to keep our roles alive.

In those precious glances and smiles I felt the bond of innocence, which is more powerful than love because it transcends love. Instead of just being here as a unit with its own private triumphs and failures, every family is a communion of souls. What we have in common isn't where we live, what schools we go to, or what we do for a living. We are sailing the seas of immortality together—that is the real bond. When you can see past the role playing and still act your role with love and dedication, then I believe you are truly spiritual in your approach to parenting.

Finally, the Seven Spiritual Laws are just ways of making this happen. They remind us how to keep the innocence flowing. There's a lot in this world that can destroy innocence and precious little that keeps it flowing. I don't look upon spiritual law as optional—this is how the universe works as it unfolds from pure, unmanifest Being to the infinite variety of the created world. If you live in tune with spiritual laws, you will be in harmony with the unlimited intelligence of Being. As parents, then, what we teach our children is no different from what we must keep teaching ourselves.

Keep the innocence flowing. It all depends on that.

Deepak Chopra has written nineteen books, which have been translated into more than thirty languages. He is also the author of more than thirty audio and videotape series, including five critically acclaimed works on public television: *Body, Mind, and Soul; The Seven Spiritual Laws of Success; The Way of the Wizard; The Crystal Cave;* and *Alchemy.* Dr. Chopra is also director of educational programs at The Chopra Center for Well Being in La Jolla, California.

Deepak Chopra and Infinite Possibilities International offer a wide range of seminars, products, and educational programs. For additional information, please contact: Infinite Possibilities International, 60 Union Avenue, Sudbury, MA 01776, U.S.A. 1-800-858-1808 (toll-free)/(508) 440-8400. For medical inquiries and health-related programs, please contact: The Chopra Center for Well Being, 7630 Fay Avenue, La Jolla, CA 92037, U.S.A. 1-888-424-6772 (toll-free)/(619) 551-7788.

Global Network for Spiritual Success
P.O. Box 2611
La Jolla, CA 92038

Dear Friend,

This book is a manifestation that emerged from thousands of
letters I received from readers of *The Seven Spiritual Laws of
Success*. Born from the same source is The Global Network for
Spiritual Success. By integrating the conscious application of the
Seven Spiritual Laws into daily life, the Network has grown into a
global family committed to the expansion of love. In concen-
trating on one law each day of the week, beginning on Sunday
with the Law of Pure Potentiality and circling into Saturday with
the Law of Dharma, we collectively harness the power of
intention to transform life on earth for ourselves and our children.

By joining the Global Network you can connect with other
members worldwide and receive inspirational and informative
materials to encourage, support, and deepen your further growth.
If you are interested in becoming a member please send a self-
addressed, stamped letter-size envelope (or an E-mail address) to
the address above. We will send you an application and a Seven
Spiritual Laws wallet card.

The Global Network for Spiritual Success is a realization of my
most cherished commitment to family. The global family is
growing, transforming, and seeking direction. I invite you to
dedicate your love and energy to the creation of a wondrous
playground for our global children. I can think of no more
satisfying an experience.

Love,

Deepak Chopra